Make Friends with Credit

understand and build a lasting relationship with good credit

Amber Rose

Taylor Rose Creations

To Brian, who taught me the art of creative lending and believed in me like no other.

To my father, who taught me my very first financial lessons.

And to my mother, my greatest support and number one fan.

Contents

INTRODUCTION

I am not a financial advisor. I did not attend a decade of university, sink into a bottomless pit of student debt, and obtain a fancy degree. I embarked on my path to financial awareness and success in 2007, when I began working for a thriving credit union in Washington State. I started as a teller, but about ten months in, I became a consumer loan officer. For those of you who don't do banking for a living, consumer loans are anything other than real estate and commercial loans. They include auto loans, credit cards, personal signature loans—that sort of thing.

It was a steep learning curve, and I didn't feel confident in my abilities (or even my choice to pursue it) until a good six months had passed. But I hit my stride, and over the next few years, I built a reputation as a knowledgeable and skilled member of the consumer lending team. My career especially took off when I moved from the busiest branch to our rapidly growing Contact Center. There I became an online loan specialist, and less than a year later, I was the first ever senior online loan specialist.

Our worlds changed in the fateful year of 2020. Our branches closed, and suddenly the Contact Center loan team became the busiest lending department in the entire credit union. Our workloads doubled or even tripled. Already a seasoned veteran, I adapted and became the top-producing member of the team. I broke every lending record of the credit union, and I remained at the top until January 2022, when I elected to leave the company and return to my hometown in Wyoming.

No amount of schooling could have taught me more than did that job. For the entire fifteen years I did it, my favorite aspect remained helping people learn, grow their credit, and achieve their financial goals. The purpose of this simple Q&A narrative is to pass that knowledge on to any who wish to learn the inner workings of the dark and mysterious world we call credit.

~Amber Rose

PART ONE: BASICS

In this first section, I will cover the basics of credit and establish context. I'll explain exactly what credit is and why it is so important in our society. Understanding is the key to success.

Q: What is credit?

A : The emphasis on an individual's credit has increased these past decades. You can hardly do anything without your credit being consulted. Want to sign up for a new cell phone plan? We need to pull your credit. Want to start a new job? We need to pull your credit. Want to rent your first apartment? We need to—you catch my drift. Your credit has become synonymous with your identity, and yet most consumers have no real idea of what it is. It seems complicated, stressful, daunting. In truth, it is quite simple.

I will demonstrate with a metaphor. Students take various classes. How well they perform in these classes is quantified by their GPA, a number that measures their academic success. The higher the GPA, the more successful the student. Credit is very similar. Consumers—people like you and me—take out various loans, which are compiled on their credit report. How well they manage (pay off) the loans is quantified by their credit score, a number that measures their success as a borrower. The higher the credit score, the more successful the borrower.

Q: What makes up my credit?

A : Credit reports are dumping grounds for financial institutions. Any time you open a loan or line of credit, your financial institution reports it to one or all of the three main credit bureaus: Experian, Equifax, and TransUnion. The bureaus compile the reported information into a comprehensive file that can be accessed by you, lenders, and other authorized institutions. Financial institutions then use this information to decide if they will lend you any money.

So, what information gets reported? The short answer is loans. Your checking and savings accounts are not reported. Your rent payments are not reported. Your cell phone bill is not reported. It is your *loan payment history* that builds your credit and provides your credit score. There is, of course, a caveat. If you stop paying your cell phone bill, or if you overdraw your checking account and don't pay that bill, it gets reported. It shows up as a negative (derogatory) item on your report and causes your score to tank.

*Helpful Tip: Experian will allow you to "self-report" your cell phone or utility bill payments. Visit Experian.com and search the word "boost." This is a useful trick for a new borrower, but be careful. New things appearing on the report of well-established borrowers can actually cause their score to drop.

Q: What's the difference between credit reports and credit scores?

A : Think of your credit report as your school report, and your credit score as your GPA. Your credit report is made up of all your loans and lines of credit, such as when you opened them, how well you pay, and how much debt you have. Your credit score is a number that lenders use to score your risk as a borrower. A high score translates into low risk, and vice versa.

Here is another metaphor. When you play a game, your performance and how well you play all add up to your high score. When you take out loans and acquire credit cards, your payment history is your performance and your credit score is your high score.

Helpful Tip: Most institutions use the terms "credit" and "credit report" interchangeably. They mean the same thing.

Q: What factors contribute to my credit score?

A : There are four main factors that go into a consumer's credit score. Each is important.

1) *Payment history*: This is most critical. Consistently making your payments on time is the most important part of good credit. Even a single late payment can drop your score fifty points or more, which can take many months to recover. Late payments also stay on your credit report for several years.

2) *Longevity*: The longer you take to pay a loan, the better it looks. Longevity establishes consistency, and a borrower who has paid well on loans for thirty years represents a lower risk than a borrower whose history only spans a few months.

3) *Balance to loan amount ratio*: The lower your owing balance compared to the original loan amount or credit limit, the better.

4). *Loan variety*: Different types of loan evaluate payment history differently. A varied portfolio is stronger than one that consists only of, say, a couple of credit cards.

*Helpful Tip: Credit scores range from 300 to 850. Lenders consider anything above about 720 to be a good score.

Q: How does my credit score affect my loan interest?

A : Credit is one of those things that won't matter to you until it matters. That's why it's so important to get started as soon as you can and get started right. Good credit translates into low interest rates, less cost, and more options. Let's break it down.

Most lenders use a *merit-based* system to determine interest rates. An interest rate indicates how much you will pay the financial institution to borrow money from it. With a few rare exceptions, there is no such thing as a zero-interest loan. A merit-based system is one that rewards high-score borrowers with low interest rates. Now let's take a look at a possible scenario.

A new borrower with no credit applies for his first auto loan. The loan is $10,000. The interest rate, called the annual percentage rate (APR), is 18.99%. This rate indicates how much the borrower will pay in interest over the course of a year. Here is the equation: loan balance x APR, or $10,000 x 18.99% (multiply $10,000 by 0.1899). In just one year, that's almost $2,000 in interest. Now consider the term of this loan. It will most likely be sixty months, or five years. As the borrower pays the loan down, the amount he pays in interest gradually decreases (this is called the amortization schedule), but that's still nearly $6,000 in interest alone! This borrower will pay more than half the loan amount in interest alone before he's done.

Now let's look at a borrower with a 760 score. She qualifies for an interest rate (APR) of 2.50%. She takes out an auto loan of $25,000 for seventy-two months, or six years. In one year, she will pay approximately $625 in interest. That's less than half of what our new borrower will pay, and the total amount in those six years is less than $2,000. For a larger loan amount and longer term, she is still paying less in interest. Remember that my numbers in these scenarios are just examples.

Have I convinced you how important a good credit score is?

Helpful Tip: You can find amortization calculators on the Internet. Simply plug "amortization calculator" into your browser's search engine. Fill in the loan amount, the interest rate, and the repayment term for a breakdown of your total cost.

PART TWO: BUILDING CREDIT

In this section, I will go over steps to get you started on your credit journey. I will give you the tools to understand the game and how to play.

Q: I have no credit. Does that mean I have good credit?

A : No. Having no credit indicates nothing to your potential lender. Sure, there's nothing bad if you have no credit. But there's also nothing to show the lender you pay your debts as agreed.

Let's return to our student metaphor. Brand-new students who have taken no classes have no grades (GPA) and therefore cannot be called good students. They are untested, untried. The same is true for new borrowers. They have never taken out a loan before and therefore cannot have good credit yet. But by following my simple steps, it is merely a matter of time until good credit is established.

*Helpful Tip: When you take out your first loan, it will be six months before your credit score is generated. Try to be patient, and remember nothing is fast in the world of credit.

Q: How do I build my credit?

A : No one is born with good credit. It takes years to build up, while a single mistake can damage it seemingly beyond repair. So how do you get started? Simple: take out a loan. It may seem a little backward, but the only way to have good credit is to be a good borrower. You can't be a borrower without a loan.

But getting started comes with an obstacle that makes it seem impossible. You apply for your first loan, but financial institutions keep turning you down because you have no credit. You find yourself stuck in a frustrating catch 22. How can you get started if no one will give you a chance? The answer is to start small.

*Helpful Tip: Begin with your local bank or credit union, which may have credit builder programs to help new borrowers get started.

Q: What's the best way to start building credit?

A : One of the best ways to start building credit is to apply for a credit card. First, a credit card will stay on your credit for as long as you keep it open. Second, cards are relatively easy to obtain. You can open a credit card practically anywhere, but make sure you do your research. Pick a card with low or no fees. Try to find one with good benefits and rewards. Look for low interest rates.

Consider opening a credit card with your local bank or credit union, which will likely have a program for new borrowers and is less likely to have hidden fees and gimmicks. You'll have to start with a small credit limit, but you may apply at any time to raise the limit and build it up over time, which is something I recommend!

It's not a bad idea to open a couple of cards. Just remember credit cards are not free money. Don't go crazy. It's easy to rack up credit card debt, but it's not an easy cycle to break. Additionally, the average repayment period of a credit card is fifteen years. That translates into thousands and thousands of dollars in interest. Do yourself a favor by never starting down that path.

Helpful Tip: For an in-depth analysis of credit cards, see Part Three. I will go into far more detail about the way to safely handle these modern conveniences.

Q: Is it important to start building credit as soon as possible?

A: Yes. When you're just setting foot in the world of adulthood, there's a lot to take in, and frankly, credit is rarely top of mind. But there are benefits to starting as soon as you can. Trust me on this. It will come to matter sooner than you think.

The most obvious benefit of building credit is the credit score. The credit score is the determining factor in the interest rate of nearly every type of loan. A new borrower who does not have a score could start off with an interest rate as much as 20% higher than that of a borrower with a good score. Allow me to put it into perspective.

Let's say borrower A has a credit score of 720. This is a solid number. Let's then say borrower A applies for an auto loan and qualifies for a rate of 2.99%. This is an attractive rate, meaning borrower A will pay much less in interest over the life of the loan. Now let us say borrower B has no credit score and applies for the same loan. Borrower B's rate is 18.99%. This is a significant difference, and not an attractive one. It means borrower B will pay far more in interest over the life of the loan.

Remember that the sooner you start, the sooner you'll get your all-important credit score. Then, when you need to apply for your first car loan, project loan, or home loan, you'll get those coveted lower rates.

Helpful Tip: For more information on lenders' requirements, see Part Three.

PART THREE: EVERYTHING YOU NEED TO KNOW ABOUT LOANS

(and possibly some stuff you didn't need to know)

In this section, we will dive into the different types of loan and the impact they have on your credit. I will also cover things lenders look for in a potential borrower and key things to consider before you apply. Finally, I will reveal all the secrets about credit cards!

Q: What are the main types of loan?

A : There are many types of loan, but they all fall into two categories: installment and revolving. They impact your credit in different ways. Let's break them down.

An installment loan is a lump sum you borrow and pay back in set monthly installments, usually over the course of several years. Once the loan is paid in full, it is closed and done. Car loans, personal loans, and home loans are all examples of installment loans.

Revolving loans have a line of credit with a set maximum limit. You can borrow up to that limit, and once the balance is paid, the maximum limit amount is replenished so you can borrow it all again. You can keep this borrow-payoff-borrow-again cycle going continuously until you decide to close the loan. Credit cards and home equity lines of credit are examples of revolving loans.

*Helpful Tip: Financial institutions prefer installment loans to revolving loans. Keep revolving debt to a minimum.

Q: What's the difference between secured and unsecured?

A : Unsecured loans are signature loans with nothing guaranteeing the loan. Credit cards, lines of credit, and personal loans are all unsecured. You agree to repay them with nothing more than your word. They are inherently riskier to lenders, so lending decisions may be more conservative.

Secured loans are backed by collateral. Cars, RVs, boats, motorcycles, and houses are all forms of collateral. They are less risky, because if you stop paying, the bank gets the collateral. This is known as *incentive to repay*.

Q: How do I apply for a loan?

A : This is the easy part. Applying simply means filling out a request for a loan. To do so, visit your local bank or credit union, physically or online, or call them. The application requires your personal information, your financial information (employer, income), and a few other odds and ends. Once you submit the application, your lender makes a decision.

One question I was asked all the time when I worked as a consumer loan officer was "Can I apply without having my credit pulled?" The answer is no. Lenders cannot complete an application without pulling your credit. Your credit report tells them how much debt you have and how well you pay it, so they cannot make a decision without that information. Make sure you're ready for the *hard pull* before you make the call.

*Helpful Tip: A "hard pull" is what lenders do when they inquire into your credit history. Too many hard pulls will cause your score to drop. See Part Four for more information.

Q: Is it good to pay a loan off quickly?

A : This is a loaded question, the answer to which is both yes and no. This is a decision only you can make, but a better question would be, what are you trying to accomplish? Let's take a look at both scenarios.

The immediate benefit to paying a loan off early is interest. The faster you pay off a loan, the less you will pay in interest, which is only accrued on your principal balance. When you make extra payments or larger payments, you're decreasing your principal balance and therefore your interest. Paying a loan off quickly reduces the total finance charge. That means, it saves you money!

The trade-off is history. The longer you take to pay off a loan, the better your credit looks. If you pay a loan off too quickly, you're not indicating much to the bureaus. Therefore, the impact it has on your credit is negligible. So, if you're trying to build credit, I recommend not paying debt off too quickly in order to maximize the impact of a steady flow of payments.

*Helpful Tip: Your lender can tell you exactly how much you will pay in interest over the life of the loan. Ask for the figures to help you decide what's best for you.

Q: What are the key things lenders look for?

A : Lenders will evaluate a number of items when reviewing your loan application.

1. *Income*: You can't get a loan without it. You must show a continual ability to repay. It can be in the form of payroll, state benefits, child support, disability, VA, and even alimony. Assets are not income. Your bank can't use your large savings account, because you could withdraw and spend it all at any time.

2. *Payment history*: Lenders try to decide whether or not to lend you money. How well you have paid off your debts is an indicator of how well you will continue to pay them off. Lenders don't have crystal balls. They can only use past trends to estimate future trends.

3. *Amounts previously borrowed*: If you're making a large request and have never had a comparable loan before, your lender will likely come back with a counter for a lower amount or require a co-signer. Remember, they evaluate future possibilities on past trends.

4. *Amount of current debt*: How much you owe right now can be a determining factor. If you have too much debt already, a

financial institution is unlikely to want to add more. This is doubly true for unsecured debt.

5. *Account history:* Building a banking relationship will yield figurative and literal dividends. You are more likely to be approved by your primary financial institution than by a lender with whom you've never done business.

Q: How much income is enough income?

A : There is no set answer to this question, but I can give you a good guideline. First, calculate your overhead. What is your rent? What are your loan payments? If this total comes to less than 40% of your monthly income, you're probably all right. This percentage is called your debt ratio, and it's more important than your actual income—within reason. Let's take a look at an example.

Our borrower has a monthly income of $2,500. Her rent is $725. Her car payment is $350. She has two credit cards, and her combined monthly payments total $85. Her monthly expenses total $1,160. To figure the debt ratio, we take $1,160 divided by $2,500. That's 46%, a bit high but not yet unreasonable.

For a concrete number, aim for 45% or lower. The more income you have, the more flexibility you have. But it is possible to obtain a loan if you have limited or fixed income.

*Helpful Tip: If you rent with a roommate, your lender will only need your portion of the rental payment.

Q: How do I know what kind of loan or service to apply for?

A : Sometimes the answer to this question is simple. If you need a new car, you apply for a car loan. But there are times when you have an end goal but only a vague notion of how to get there. Don't worry. You don't need to know the ins and outs of banking. I recommend calling your financial institution rather than trying to apply online.

Start by explaining your problem: "I have too many credit card payments." This establishes a baseline. Then explain what you want to accomplish—for example, "I want lower monthly payments!" Your lender can then give you your options. Let your financial institution be the expert. It's not your job to exhaustively research loans and banking and products to determine what's best for you.

*Helpful Tip: Don't be afraid to ask lenders if their recommendation is the lowest possible interest rate. Remember you want the best rate and lowest cost. This is your money!

Q: Why do different loans have different interest rates?

A : You may have noticed that auto loans have lower rates than personal loans. A financial institution offers lower rates on loans with inherently less risk. Let's start with personal loans.

Personal loans, also called signature loans, are unsecured amounts your financial institution lends you and trusts you to pay back. This comes with quite a bit of risk, since if you fail to pay, your financial institution will likely never recoup the loss. Therefore, the rates are high to help mitigate the risk. You may see them as high as 18% –25%.

Now let's look at auto loans. Auto loans have nice, low rates. That's because there's less inherent risk. If you fail to pay, the bank gets the car. There's potential to recoup some of the loss. After all, financial institutions are businesses, so they do have to consider their well-being.

Let's move on to RV loans. Though an RV loan is secured by the travel trailer or the motorhome, this type of vehicle is called *leisure collateral*. If something happens in your life, you're less likely to pay off your toy than your daily driver. So while this type of loan will have better rates than a personal loan, it's still not as low as an auto loan. This is also true of boats and off-road vehicles such as ATVs, UTVs, snowmobiles, and dirt bikes.

*Helpful Tip: There are always times when financial institutions have special promotions that may contradict what I've laid out. Try to take advantage of them!

Q: I qualify only for a high interest rate. Should I just pay in cash?

A : If you're a new borrower, high interest rates are a fact of life. This can make taking out a loan a very unattractive proposition. After all, you don't want to pay thousands and thousands in interest. I do not recommend avoiding the loan altogether, and here's why.

The longer you put off your first loan, the more likely you are to be declined when you really need a loan. You need to start building credit some time. Take a deep breath and take the plunge, and be comforted by the fact that there is light at the end of the tunnel.

When you are a new borrower, have no credit score, and are applying for your first car loan, you will qualify only for a high rate. I won't pretend otherwise. Take heart. You do not have to settle for that rate for the entire five or six years of the loan! As I mentioned in previous sections, your credit score will appear after six months. If you have paid well so far, it will be a solid number. You may then apply to reduce your interest rate. It could drop as much as 10%! This is a huge savings, and most financial institutions won't charge you any fees for doing this.

Helpful Tip: You can apply for a rate change on any type of loan, not just an auto loan.

Q: What's the deal with credit cards?

A : As promised, I will now dive deep into the murky waters of credit cards. There is a lot of misinformation floating around out there, and much of it is contradictory. As a result, many borrowers develop apprehension. Credit cards have become surprisingly necessary in our society, and there is cause to approach them with a measure of caution. Uniquely, they are the only kind of loan that can hurt your credit even if you always make your payments on time.

But there is nothing to fear. Credit cards, as I mentioned in Part Two, are a great way to build credit. You just need to follow a few easy rules. First and most obviously, always make your payments on time. Second, never max out your credit card.

Now, here's where I'm sure you've heard conflicting advice, most likely along the lines of maxing out the card and paying it off every month. My recommendation is to stop listening to bad advice. I am not advising you. I am telling you how to maximize a credit card's positive impact on your credit.

Q: How do I use a credit card?

A : Before I answer that, there is one thing I'd like to make inescapably clear. A credit card is a *loan*. It is not free money. It is not a buy-now-pay-later program. Falling into credit card debt is the most common mistake borrowers—new and veteran—make. Here's a good rule of thumb: if you *need* a credit card because you *need* the money, you probably shouldn't get one.

Now, back to the question at hand. Whatever the credit card company and whatever your limit, never carry a balance on the card. You've probably heard somewhere that you need to keep a balance on the card for it to look good on your credit. This simply isn't true. The credit bureaus don't care if you never carry a balance. They only care if you pay on time and if you carry a high balance.

Some sources advise keeping the balance below 30% of the credit limit. For example, if you have a credit limit of $1,000, never spend more than $300 before paying the balance down/off. If you want to use a concrete formula, pick an even lower number, such as 15%. The lower the better. Here is my personal method: I use a card to pay for my groceries. I log into my mobile banking service and immediately transfer the cash from my checking account to the card. That way I get the card rewards but don't have to worry about the balance. Remember: the lower your credit card utilization, the better!

There's another benefit to never carrying a balance. Unlike any other type of loan, credit cards do not accrue interest if you always pay the debt in full. As long as your full statement balance is paid by your due date, no interest is charged. I consider this a pretty strong incentive to pay off the card!

One thing to keep in mind: I don't recommend never using your card. Some institutions will close your card if it goes inactive too long. Use your cards a couple times a year or so just to keep them awake and alive. Don't forget that having an open loan on your credit for years and years looks great.

So, why do the bureaus penalize you for maxing out your credit cards? They treat maxed out cards as indicators that you are trying to live outside your means and supplement your income.

Helpful Tip: You do not need to wait until your due date to pay your credit card. You can pay it off as soon as you use it. This is another reason I recommend applying for a card with your local bank or credit union. You can pay it right in the financial institution's mobile app or with a quick phone call.

Q: Does closing a credit card hurt my credit?

A : Yes and no. Yes, because closing a line of credit will most likely cause your score to drop. No, because it's not a negative thing. Let's break it down.

Remember how in Part One I said credit scores are partly based on the length of time an account has been established? If you keep a credit card open for decades, that looks great. It means you've successfully managed the card all that time. If you suddenly close it, you're closing out all that beautiful payment history, and that's why your score drops.

It is important to note that your lower score is not necessarily a negative thing. It just means you changed something. I do not recommend closing out a credit card unless you have a major problem with overspending on it, or you do not like the fees.

Q: I've never gotten an auto loan before. What should I know?

A : Most new borrowers feel intimidated by the prospect of buying their first car. This is doubly true if a dealership is involved. After all, these guys have quite a bad reputation. The truth is, with a little preparation and research you'll be car shopping like a pro.

Tip #1) *Know which car you want*: Do not go to a car lot with no vehicle in mind. Not only could this add hours to your time on the lot, but it could lead to major overspending. Searching for cars online is easy and doesn't even require getting off your couch. Your local bank or credit union may even have a resource for this. The credit union where I worked had a link to all its participating dealerships, making it very easy for our members to search their inventory. Others may have the same.

Tip #2) *Find the car's true value*: When you find a car you like, go to a vehicle valuation site such as the Kelley Blue Book or J. D. Power (formerly NADA) to look up the car's value. You don't want to pay more than it's worth.

Tip #3) *Tax and license fee*: Don't forget to budget for tax and a licensing fee. Each state will have different fees, so make sure you account for them. They can add thousands of dollars to your loan. Your local bank or credit union can also tell you exactly how much to expect.

Tip #4) *Insurance*: Financial institutions will require you to carry full coverage—comprehensive and collision—for the life of the loan. Make sure to do your research and ensure you can afford both the car loan payment and the insurance payment. If you fail to keep the vehicle insured, your financial institution will add a protection to your loan, and the fees will be steep.

Tip #5) *Extended warranties*: Think carefully before accepting any extended warranties beyond the factory warranty. It can cost thousands of dollars. That's a lot of negative equity, meaning that your loan will be much higher than the vehicle's value. Not only can this increase your interest rate with your bank but it automatically puts you in a weak position. Some dealerships may even tell you your bank or credit union won't approve the loan without a warranty. I have never known this to be true.

Tip #6) *Budget*: Have a budget and stick to it. Dealerships are businesses; they want to protect their bottom line. Don't let it be at your expense.

Tip #7) *Avoid temptation*: Don't let your eyes be bigger than your stomach, so to speak. It's easy to let yourself get swept away by a fancy, shiny car. The average repayment period of an auto loan is seven years. The novelty of the shiny car will wear off long before the loan is paid.

Tip #8) *Down payment*: Save up a down payment. Even having a couple thousand set aside will help.

Tip #9) *Beware the small print*: Read your documents carefully! Make sure to pay especial attention to the retail installment contract. *Do not* let yourself get suckered into added fees. Once you've signed, it's a done deal. Make sure you sign for exactly what you wanted and not one penny more.

Tip #10) *Don't be afraid to say no*: If the car is not what you want, just walk away. Don't settle for less. You'll find the deal that's right for you.

Q: Can I buy a car from an individual rather than a dealership?

A : Yes. This is known as a private party sale, and it comes with a slightly different set of rules and challenges. Just as there are for a dealer purchases, there are a few things you need to know.

Tip #1) *Scammers*: When you purchase a car from a private party, you're more likely to encounter a scammer than you would at a dealership. If you're searching online sites such as Craigslist or Facebook, make sure you do not volunteer any information about yourself. Scrutinize cash-only offers closely. Sellers should be aware that buyers may need to finance, and this means a bank draft or cashier's check, both of which are guaranteed funds.

Tip #2) *VIN and branding*: Look for the vehicle identification number (VIN). Ask your lender to run it and make sure it's a clean title. Most financial institutions won't finance cars with branded titles. A brand indicates something wrong in the car's past—for example, it's been salvaged or rebuilt. I recommend avoiding rebuilt cars, which likely were wrecked, totaled, and then patched back up. There is no standard for rebuilding a car, which means there's no guarantee of quality of work.

Tip #3) *Tax and licensing fees*: These are still due in a private party sale. Don't forget to budget for them.

Tip #4) *Insurance*: This is still a requirement. Another thing to keep in mind is that some insurance companies won't insure rebuilt cars, which is one more reason to avoid them.

Tip #5) *Title transfer*: You and your seller may have to physically visit your local bank or credit union to complete title transfer paperwork because these documents often require a notary's signature. Therefore, it's a good idea to find a seller near you to avoid logistics debacles.

Tip #6) *After-market add-ons*: Sometimes, sellers put after-market features on their vehicles such as stereo and audio systems and fancy tires, among other things. They will sell the car for what they think it's worth and try to recoup their money. Your lender won't care about those things, which, contrary to popular opinion, don't increase the value of a car/truck. Therefore, in these situations, you will likely have to pay some money out of your pocket.

*Helpful Tip: Every state has its own requirements when it comes to tax and title documents. Ask your local bank or credit union for your state's specific rules.

Q: What do lenders look for when you ask for a car loan?

A : Your lender's requirements will directly affect your search. Here are a few key things to keep in mind.

Item #1) *Value of vehicle*: I recommended previously that you look up the value of the vehicle you want to purchase. Financial institutions will have caps on the amount you may borrow as compared to the value, which is called the loan-to-value ratio (LTV). This should only make sense. You can't get a $50,000 loan on a car that's only worth $10,000. A stronger borrower will be approved for a higher LTV, but it's a good idea to keep that ratio as low as possible. You don't want to pay more than a car is worth! To calculate the LTV, here is the formula: loan amount divided by value. A loan of $25,000 on a car worth $25,000 is 100%. A loan of $25,000 on a car worth $30,000 is 83.33%. A loan of $25,000 on a car worth $20,000 is 125%.

Item #2) *Age of vehicle*: Older vehicles begin to decline in value. At twenty years, their value depreciates steeply. Some financial institutions won't lend on a vehicle older than seven years.

Item #3) *Mileage of vehicle*: Not only does a high mileage decrease the vehicle's value but it also increases the risk to you and your lender. A car with high mileage is more likely to need maintenance soon. Will you be able to afford a repair bill of a few thousand dollars? Your lender will consider that. So should you.

Q: What is a cosigner, and what is a coborrower?

A : The distinction between these two is subtle. Cosigners are basically guarantors. They are not responsible for making payments unless the primary borrower stops paying. Then the financial institution will collect on the cosigner. In a loan application, the borrower and cosigner are evaluated individually, and their income is not combined on the application.

A coborrower is an equal owner of the debt, sharing equal liability for payments. In a loan application, borrower and coborrower are evaluated together, and their income is combined in the application. Therefore, if you were declined due to insufficient income, you need a coborrower and not a cosigner.

There are some important things to note. First, a cosigner is not a fix-it patch. If a borrower has very poor credit, presenting a cosigner is not a guarantee of approval. Second, lenders do not differentiate between a cosigner and a coborrower if you are trying to apply for a new loan and have cosigned for someone. For example, let's say you cosigned an auto loan for your child and now you want to apply for your own auto loan. Your lender will not care that you are just a cosigner on your child's loan. The fact is that you could be liable for making payments on your child's loan counts against you. Keep that in mind if you're considering cosigning.

Helpful Tip: Payments and late payments affects the credit of cosigners and coborrowers the same. Financial institutions will not notify a cosigner of a late payment until attempts to collect payment from the primary borrower have failed. This can take one or even two months by which time the late payment has already been reported to the bureaus and your score has dropped. Consider being a coborrower. Your financial institution will then notify you long before the late payment is reported.

Q: Can I, as a coborrower, remove my name from a loan?

A : No. Loans are a contract, approved with two people, two credit reports, and two incomes. Removing a borrower requires a brand-new evaluation of the remaining borrower who must apply for and qualify for a new loan in his/her name alone and sign all new documentation.

It is also important to note that a divorce decree does not have anything to do with a loan. Let's say coborrower A and coborrower B get divorced. The court awards their car to coborrower A. This applies only to the actual property and not the loan. To remove coborrower B, coborrower A would have to apply for a new car loan in his/her name only. Coborrower A would not have to get permission from coborrower B to do so, however. Nor would coborrower B have to sign any loan documents for this transaction.

Helpful Tip: This is also true for co-signers. The primary borrower would still have to apply for the loan in just their name.

Q: My bank turned me down! What gives?

A : Here's the best advice I can give you: Don't take it personally. A loan application is a complex tapestry, and lenders have to make sure each thread is in the right place. It's a numbers game, and decisions have nothing to do with you personally.

Believe it or not, financial institutions are tightly regulated. If they offer you a loan you cannot afford, that's called predatory lending. This is a violation of certain federal regulations, and the institution can be held criminally liable for that.

Ask your lender for the exact reasons you were declined. Ask for the precise steps to rectify the situation. Follow through. Remember your bank didn't turn you down because it doesn't like you. Banks have auditors to whom they must answer.

*Helpful Tip: Financial institutions want to lend to you! Each funded loan translates into dollars for them, so it's in their best interest to approve borrowers.

PART FOUR: EVENING THE SCORE

I n this section, I will discuss the various ways your actions affect your credit score. What causes it to drop can be a mystery, so I will shed a little light on the subject.

Q: Why did my score drop?

A : If you closely monitor your credit score, you will notice it can fluctuate every single month. Any changes at all can make it go up or down a few points. This is nothing to worry about, it's completely normal. Let's take a look at a scenario.

Our borrower has a credit score of 800, which is a great number, with no outstanding debts, late payments, and collections on four credit cards, none of which have had a balance in the last year. Our borrower uses one of these credit cards and a balance of $300 is reported to the bureau. The credit score drops to 780. Harsh, right? It seems as if the credit bureau is penalizing our borrower for using the card. This isn't strictly true. Nor is it a negative thing. It just means something changed. That's why, in Part Three in my segment on credit cards, I recommended always paying the card's balance as soon as you use it. Keep in mind that my numbers here are just examples and don't reflect what could actually happen.

*Helpful Tip: Monitoring your credit score and taking note of any change is a good thing! It could alert you to potential fraudulent activity.

Q: Why does it matter if I make a late payment?

A : Bad things happen. Sometimes life feels like one string of disasters after another. It can feel as if your bank holds it against you. So, why the heavy emphasis? Well, simply put, a pattern of late payments can indicate financial distress, and your bank is legally obligated to ensure it doesn't make your situation worse by adding more payments.

If you find yourself in a tight spot, reach out to your financial institution. Don't be embarrassed. That kind of thing happens to us all! Your bank or credit union will most likely have programs in place to allow you to skip a payment without the dreaded delinquency showing up on your credit report. This will keep you in good standing and prevent a negative impact on your credit score.

Helpful Tip: Most loans have a grace period before you're considered past due. For example, if your due date is the tenth of the month, you will have until the twentieth to make your payment before a late fee is assessed. You are not reported as delinquent on your credit report until you're thirty days past due.

Q: Why do too many inquiries cause my score to drop?

A : As I mentioned earlier, the credit bureaus will start penalizing you if there are too many inquiries (reviews of your credit history). An inquiry occurs any time you apply for a new loan or line of credit and is sometimes called a hard pull or hard hit. It indicates to the bureaus that you are seeking a loan. There are many legitimate reasons a borrower may need to apply for a loan, but too many can suggest shopping for credit. By and large, an individual constantly looking for loans poses a greater risk than one who does not.

Helpful Tip #1: Shopping for credit simply means opening too many credit cards at once. Remember, this can indicate you're looking for a way to supplement your income with a loan.

Helpful Tip #2: Inquiries stay on your credit report for two years, after which time they drop off. Your credit report will show where the inquiry came from, so it's very easy for a potential lender to tell if you were car shopping or applying for store credit cards.

Q: Does taking out a new loan cause my score to drop?

A : Yes. It's important to recognize this isn't a negative thing, and it ties directly into what we covered in Part One: the factors that contribute to your credit score. When you take out a new loan, let's say a $15,000 auto loan, your owing balance and the original loan amount are the same. As you make your monthly payments, your owing balance goes down and the gap between it and the original loan amount grows. Your score will go up as that happens.

The length of time accounts have been established also comes into play. A brand-new loan hasn't been established very long, so your score drops. Don't forget this is a temporary state. Your score will begin to bounce back, especially if you have a solid foundation of a good payment history.

Q: I can see my score online. Why is it different from the one pulled by my bank?

A : This is an especially confusing aspect of credit. These days, it's relatively easy to obtain your credit score. Your bank or credit union might provide it each month. Your credit card companies might. There are sites devoted to it. You can even go straight to the bureaus to acquire your score. And then you apply for a loan only to be told your score is twenty points lower than what you saw online!

Each bureau will have its own scoring method. To further complicate the issue, these scoring methods will have multiple platforms, all of which will generate a different number. The unfortunate truth is that financial institutions will often use the harshest scoring method for the most accurate score. There's nothing we can do about that. But it's a good rule of thumb to estimate that the score lenders use will be twenty points lower.

*Helpful Tip: When your local bank or credit union provides you with a monthly credit score, this is not an inquiry. Nor does it come from your bank or credit union. The number is received in a report from the credit bureau, which is passed along to you as a courtesy. It does not affect your score.

Q: I pay well, but my score is low. Please explain!

A : The number-one cause of a score that seems too low is credit card debt. If you have a perfect payment history on your home loan, auto loans, and credit cards, look at your credit card utilization. Do you have high balances compared to the credit limits? Pay those bad boys down. You will see your score jump during the next reporting cycle.

Your score could also be low if you have a new loan, if you refinanced your auto or home loan, or if there are quite a few inquiries in a short period of time.

Of course, a low score can also be an indicator of something amiss. That's why it's important to monitor your credit to make sure there's nothing there that shouldn't be. It's easier than ever for criminals to obtain your information, so a low score could be a red flag.

*Helpful Tip: Take advantage of your free annual credit report. Visit the credit bureau websites directly or go to annualcreditreport.com. If you're still not sure how to obtain it, contact your local bank or credit union, which can point you in the right direction.

PART FIVE: TIDYING UP

In this section, I will cover some of the less pleasant aspects of credit. You'll find useful info and tips for cleaning up negative items or handling all that outstanding debt.

Q: I have collections on my credit. What should I do?

A : Collections happen to the best of us. They can seem like an insurmountable obstacle. They don't need to be. Before we discuss reconciling a collection, let's go over the basics.

A collection is a debt incurred with a financial institution, a utility company, or a hospital (to name a few). When a borrower neglects to pay, this debt is sold to a third party known as a collection agency. It becomes a collection, and the agency will then collect any payment on the debt.

You've probably heard that collections fall off your credit after seven years. Strictly speaking, this is true. But collections can have a significant negative impact not only on your score but also your chances of getting a new loan. When you need a new car, you won't have seven years to wait.

The best practice is to pay the collection off as quickly as you can. Most collection agencies will also *settle* the debt. This involves paying one lump sum—usually 50% of the original debt —and the rest is written off. This shows the collection as settled rather than unpaid on your credit report, and your score will slowly begin to creep back up. Lenders view borrowers who settle debt more favorably than those who simply ignore their obligations.

Helpful Tip: Pulling credit on yourself (soft pull) will give you the collection agency's information, dates, and account numbers to make it easier for you to reconcile. Pulling credit on yourself does not hurt your score or show up on the report as an inquiry.

Q: I have a ton of credit card debt. What should I do?

A : Debt consolidation! This is a personal passion of mine. Consolidating your credit cards in one installment loan comes with massive benefits. Let's break them down.

Benefit #1) *Lower monthly expense*: Typically speaking, fifteen credit card payments will total more than one installment loan payment. Your monthly expense, therefore, drops.

Benefit #2) *Lower interest rate*: Most installment loans have lower interest rates than credit cards. The average interest rate of a credit card is over 20%. You could potentially pay half that on an installment loan.

Benefit #3) *Faster payoff*: As I already mentioned, the average repayment period of a credit card is fifteen years. The average repayment period of an installment loan is four to five years. You'll have your debt paid off in a third of the time!

Benefit #4) *Better score with paid-off balances*: Maxed out credit cards hurt your credit. Paying them all off will help your score begin to recover and sometimes the result is immediate!

Benefit #5) *Positive lender response*: Lenders view installment loans more favorably than credit card debt. Your chances of approval are higher if you don't have balances on all your cards.

Now, there is a caveat. Installment loans are unsecured. If you owe $15,000 in credit card debt, and you apply for a $15,000 consolidation loan, that's a fair amount unsecured. As I previously mentioned, lenders may be more conservative with decisions on unsecured loans. Don't worry, I have a solution for you: consider securing your loan.

Let's say you own your truck outright, and it is worth $25,000. Instead of applying for an unsecured loan, apply for an auto loan against the equity of your truck. The lender holds the title until the loan is paid. A secured loan comes with even more benefits.

Benefit #1) *Even lower rates*: Secured loans have even *lower* interest rates for even *greater* savings.

Benefit #2) *Longer repayment terms*: Secured loans offer longer repayment terms, dropping your monthly expense even lower.

Benefit #3) *Greater chance of approval*: Lenders view secured loans more favorably than unsecured, greatly increasing your chances of approval.

See the next question for how to consolidate debts if your financial institution still declines you.

Helpful Tip: Using your vehicle as collateral in this type of scenario is still an auto loan. Therefore, your lender will require you to carry full-coverage insurance for the life of the loan.

Q: Should I work with a debt management company?

A : Yes. Before I discuss best practice, let me give you a quick explanation of what I mean. Debt management or financial counseling companies offer services such as making payment arrangements with your creditors, offering financial advice, budget planning and management, and helping you prepare for major life events. These can be a great help, especially if you have negative items on your credit you want to clean up.

Now a word of caution: not all companies are created equal. Don't perform an online search and pick the first one that pops up. Some will charge you exorbitant fees, some may be dishonest, and some may even be fraudulent.

Reach out to your local bank or credit union to ask for direction. Chances are your financial institution can guide you to a known and trusted company and may even have an internal resource for you.

*Helpful Tip: Never be too ashamed or embarrassed to ask for help! Your local bank or credit union is there for you and is sure to have passionate employees who—as I do—want to help you better your financial situation.

Q: I hear so many horror stories about identity theft. Should I freeze my credit?

A : That's up to you. But freezing your credit can prevent fraudsters from taking out loans in your name. Simply put, freezing your credit means no one can pull your credit until you unfreeze it. Since no financial institution will offer a loan without a credit report, freezing credit protects you from unauthorized activity. Visit the bureaus' sites directly and search for "place freeze" or "manage freeze."

Unfreezing your credit is quick and easy. Go back to the bureaus' sites and do the exact same thing but in reverse.

I think a better question is why *wouldn't* you freeze you credit?

Helpful Tip: You can also place a fraud alert on your credit, but this is less secure and only requires a lender to exercise more caution in identifying the borrower. It does not prevent your credit from being pulled.

Q: Is it possible to have perfect credit?

A : Yes! Most emphatically yes. It is possible to go through your entire life without a single blemish on your credit report. Avoid common mistakes such as treating credit cards as free money or cosigning for a friend. Start small, consider your choices carefully, and plan ahead.

It is also possible to repair any damaged credit. Utilize your local bank or credit union's resources, don't be afraid to ask for help, and don't get discouraged. You can do it. Anyone can. During my career as a lender, I helped one family take their credit scores from the low 500s to high 800s. All they did was follow my simple steps. It took them several years, but they ended up in the home of their dreams. That sort of thing is attainable for anyone.

Always remember it can take decades to build up excellent credit. It can take seconds to ruin it. Be patient, be wise, and don't be afraid. Credit can smell fear.

"Building credit is a marathon, not a 100-meter dash." ~My sister

Final Thoughts

On your credit journey, never decide not to care. You don't need to agonize over it while you're young, but poor decisions can ruin your credit before you even start. You may not care when you're nineteen, but when you need to buy your first car or home, you will—in a big way. Poor credit translates into high interest rates, high payments, and fewer options. Financial institutions are less likely to give you a chance when you have colorful history.

Remember it's easier to build good credit than repair damaged credit. Take care of it, and it will take care of you.

GLOSSARY

E ver wondered what those confusing banker terms mean? Wonder no more!

Glossary of Terms

- Adverse action: lender's negative response. A financial institution makes a decision adverse to your request. This is fancy terminology for declining or turning down a loan request.

- Amortization: a loan's repayment schedule. Basically, this is the breakdown of your monthly payments over the loan's term, including how much goes to interest and how much goes to principal.

- APR: annual percentage rate, also called interest rate. This is the amount of interest you will pay over the course of a year.

- Branded title: indicator of something wrong with the vehicle, usually that it was totaled and then rebuilt.

- Closed-ended loan: see Installment loan.

- Coborrower: joint borrower on a loan, an equal owner of the debt. Financial institutions can collect on both/all borrowers.

- Cosigner: guarantor on a loan. Financial institutions will not collect on a cosigner unless the primary borrower cannot or will not pay.

- Collateral: anything used to secure a loan. It can be money in your savings account or a car/boat/RV.

- Consumer: *You*! Every individual is a consumer.

- Counteroffer: alternative offer. When lenders don't approve a request, they may offer something different, such as a smaller loan or shorter term.

- Debt ratio: monthly payments compared to monthly income. To calculate, add up your monthly payments and divide by your monthly income. Utilities and cell phone bills are not included, only loan payments.

- Default: past due loan payment indicating you are not in good standing with your lender.

- Delinquency: late or missed payments.

- Derogatory: negative report on something such as a charge-off or collection.

- Discretionary income: what's left after all your loan payments have come out.

- Dispute: also called a credit dispute, this is when something is wrong on your credit, such as a loan you didn't open, and you ask the credit bureaus to look into it and correct the issue. You cannot dispute items on your credit with financial institutions, only with the credit bureaus.

- Equal Credit Opportunity Act (ECOA): federal regulation that prohibits financial institutions from discriminatory behavior based on race, color, religion, national origin, sex, marital status, and age.

- Equity: available value of collateral (see Collateral). If you owe less than your collateral's worth, you have positive equity. If you owe more than it's worth, you have negative equity.

- Finance charge: amount of interest paid on a loan. The total finance charge is the sum over the life of the loan. Often, if you pay a loan off early, you will reduce the finance charge. Most financial institutions do not impose early payoff penalties.

- Financial institution: organizations including, but not limited to, banks and credit unions.

- Front-end LTV: see LTV.

- Hard pull/hard hit: lender's review of your credit history, which indicates you are applying, or have applied, for a loan.

It shows up on your credit as an inquiry, and too many of them can cause your score to drop.

• Installment loan: set amount you borrow and repay in monthly installments following a prearranged schedule.

• Loan-to-value (LTV): amount you borrow compared to the value of your collateral (see Collateral). Here is the simple formula: loan amount divided by collateral value. For example, a loan of $10,000 on a vehicle worth $8,000 is an LTV of 125%. The front-end LTV (FELTV) is the sale price of the vehicle compared to the value before any tax/licensing is added.

• Maturity: end of loan's term; date when the last payment is made.

• Open-ended loan: see Revolving loan.

• Origination fees: fees imposed by a financial institution for taking out a loan. They are not common on consumer loans but usually charged on commercial or real estate loans.

• Per diem: daily interest accrual. To calculate: loan balance x APR/365 (days in a year). For example, for a loan of $10,000 with an APR of 3.24%, the per diem would be $0.89.

• Predatory lending: loans approved for people who cannot afford them or loans with excessive fees.

• Prepayment penalty: fee imposed by a financial institution for paying a loan off early.

• Principal balance: amount owed before any interest is added/accrued.

• Revolving loan: line of credit with a set limit that is replenished with each payment until the borrower elects to close the loan.

• Risk: likelihood of payment problems. A financial institution defines a low risk borrower as someone who has little to no history of delinquency or payment issues.

• Secured loan: a loan with collateral. These include auto loans, home loans, RV loans, savings loans, and boat loans.

- Security: added layer of security that the loan will be paid back. The extra security is usually provided by collateral.

- Settle: settling a debt means arranging with a debtor to pay back a lump sum (usually 50%) all at once so the debt/collection no longer shows as unpaid.

- Soft pull (also called soft hit, soft inquiry): self-review of credit. When you pull credit on yourself, this is called a soft pull. It does not come with a credit score and is not used for a loan application. It does not show up on your credit report and will not affect your score. Renters, utility companies, and cell phone companies may do a soft pull when you apply for your first apartment, utility, or phone program. Consumers pull credit on themselves to make sure everything is fine or if they need to research items for disputes.

- Term: length of a loan's repayment schedule, usually in months. For example, if you take out a car loan for five years, that's a sixty-month term.

- Tradeline: fancy word for a loan on your credit report. You will only ever hear bankers use it.

- Unsecured debt ratio: sum of unsecured debt compared to annual income. This is typically made up of credit card debt. Here is a simple formula: sum of unsecured debt divided by annual income. For example, if you owe $25,000 in credit card debt and have an annual income of $50,000, that's a 50% unsecured debt ratio.

About Author

Amber Rose was born in Washington but raised in Wyoming. She moved back to Washington after obtaining her AA degree, and she entered the banking world in 2007. She worked in consumer loans for almost fifteen years, a career which instilled a passion for educating new borrowers about the inner workings of credit and loans. In December of 2021, she decided to leave her job and move back to her hometown in Wyoming to be closer to her family. The passion for educating came with her, prompting the decision to write this book.

You can find her online at ambertaylorrose.com.